pray the
scriptures
when life hurts

pray the
scriptures

when life hurts

Experience Hope and Healing
Through the Power of God's Word

kevin johnson

BETHANY HOUSE PUBLISHERS
a division of Baker Publishing Group
Minneapolis, Minnesota

Published by Bethany House Publishers
11400 Hampshire Avenue South
Bloomington, Minnesota 55438
www.bethanyhouse.com

Bethany House Publishers is a division of
Baker Publishing Group, Grand Rapids, Michigan

Printed in the United States of America

Library of Congress Cataloging-in-Publication Data is on file at the Library of Congress, Washington, DC.

ISBN 978-0-7642-1230-7

14   15   16   17   18   19   20   7   6   5   4   3   2   1

To Lyn
For worse or for better
Always my love

contents

1

dream

I knew I needed help when I dreamed I killed myself.

I had long tried to navigate a grim life situation I felt I could neither escape nor change. By day I twisted in pain. By night I tossed in anguish, rarely sleeping more than three or four hours. Several times a week I screamed in my sleep. My wife and I at least found dark humor in her attempts to rouse me from my nightmares. Lyn slapped me. Or pulled away my pillow and let my head drop. Or hosed me with a spray bottle she kept ready on her nightstand. After a while even a shot of water in my face lost its surprise, and I would lie in bed awake but not awake, paralyzed and terrified, until I jolted to full alertness. After many months, my lack of sleep led to exhaustion, then depression, and finally despair.

Years before, I had helped lead a group where hurting students could get and give support. Each week I watched other staff members skillfully coax youth to open up, asking them to start by sharing a one-word feeling and rate their week from a 10—amazing—to a 0—wretched.

I came up with my own personal scoring system. For years I rarely rose above a mildly happy 6 or 5 . . . 4 was a grinding day-to-day existence . . . 3 meant I wished I could curl up and die . . . 2 meant I was thinking if and how I could make that happen . . . and 1 meant I was on the verge of ending my life. Most months I lived at a 3. For weeks at a time I wavered around a 2. At times I sunk close to a 1.

Mind

I woke from that dream that I had taken my life just as my consciousness was fading away. It was a long time before I told Lyn—my soul mate—about my nightmare. As a pastor I looked around and saw few safe places to bare my soul—not bosses, not co-workers, not church members. I worried about scaring family and friends. So I went to my doctor.

I counseled hurting people all the time. I did what I told them to do when I referred them to specialized help. Cut the crap. Get to the point. No one can x-ray what goes on in your head. You have to speak up. So I handed my physician a list of everything I was thinking and feeling. Some of those blunt realities:

- *I'm in a bad situation that takes enormous energy to face day after day.*
- *Every day brings some new situation that feels like being stabbed by a knife.*
- *We're all suffering but suffering alone.*
- *I don't get joy out of things that should overjoy me.*
- *I could nap at any moment, but if I lie down I feel too agitated to rest.*

- *I want to eat all the time. I have gained thirty pounds in the last eighteen months.*
- *I tell Lyn to hit me over the head with a brick—to make this stop.*
- *I have really good coping skills but still feel deep pain inside.*
- *I have gone from thinking my feelings are a reaction to stress to seeing them as something dark inside me that won't go away.*
- *I think about dying and suicide, but at this time I'm still able to get back to a purely rational response—that death isn't an appropriate response to the situation. These thoughts have been going on for months.*

Everything boiled down to one statement:

- *What keeps me going—what keeps me alive—is Lyn and the kids.*

My doctor offered a concise summary: "Obviously, you're depressed." With his simple words he acknowledged where I was at. He promised that I didn't have to stay there.

Body

For more than a year I fought my way back from mental and emotional despair. But when my head was finally in a better place, my body broke. One morning I felt something like a cell phone vibrating on my calf. Not a phantom ring but an actual buzz. My doctor said it was probably a fasciculation, like an eye twitch but in a different spot. If it got worse, he would send me to a neurologist.

It got worse. Within a week I noticed twitching, buzzing, and electrical sensations all over my body. I felt random freezing and burning. I jumped at piercing needle stabs. At times my feet felt wet, like I was sloshing through a puddle. Constant spasms in my arches looked like worms crawling under my skin. I was weak and scared.

After a tense physical exam with Lyn watching, the first thing out of the neurologist's mouth was "ALS"—amyotrophic lateral sclerosis, often called Lou Gehrig's disease—a degenerative nerve death that could cause the symptoms I was experiencing. For most of the summer doctors and technicians scanned and poked me. They sent shocks down my legs and arms to measure nerve velocity. They stuck me with needles and listened for muscle noise. I learned that neurologists are known as "vampires" because of the quantities of blood they draw to rule out possible ailments.

Lyn and I knew people who had died of ALS. We happened to know two more who were trapped in rapidly failing bodies even as their minds remained perfectly clear, and we began to anticipate that fate. But in the early fall I got a nonlethal diagnosis—benign fasciculation. It's an annoyance that recent tests again confirmed.

I got my diagnosis in September. Then came October. After more than a week of what seemed like a virus or influenza, I went to an emergency room with a wildly fluctuating fever that one afternoon had left me shaking uncontrollably. At the moment I didn't look sick enough to be in the ER and was almost sent home—until my white blood count signaled a dire infection. After a few days in the hospital on antibiotics (and loaded up with hydrocodone and morphine), I felt pretty swell. I wanted to go home. Then a surgeon got in my face and told me I needed to chain myself to the wall until my team figured out exactly why I was sick and how to treat it. They discovered a sack of infection the size of a tennis ball, a freak abscess in and around my liver.

I stayed in the hospital a few more days and went home with a drain sticking out my side. In late November I emerged from a fog of illness and drugs to realize I easily could have died. In December the drain was removed and I finished a long course of antibiotics. By January I was well enough to have my gallbladder cut out, a bonus from having my abdomen closely scrutinized. Coming out of anesthesia was rough. If there's a video floating around called "Pastors Behaving Badly," I've warned you. By April I was starting to feel normal. Whatever that is.

The fact that life hurts has never been abstract for me—theoretical, unfelt, detached from reality. When I was in middle school my mom barely survived cancer. I later watched my dad grow weary as a lifelong inner-city schoolteacher. I grew up in the best of families—nevertheless in the shadow of tragedy, illness, and death. But my own adult experiences have marked me most deeply. Compared to the pains that many people endure—maybe what you face daily—they amount to nothing. But I've realized firsthand that life hurts. Inside. Out. Body. Soul. And I've observed people long enough to realize that sooner or later we all face pain up close. It's the difference between seeing a storm in the distance and getting struck by lightning.

Prayer

I've been trained to overcome stress. I've counseled people through mind-blowing evil. I've spent years studying and teaching Scripture. I wish I could say my professional and personal background gave me everything I needed to withstand emotional, mental, and physical trauma. But when I read that "the Lord gives sleep to those he loves" (Psalm 127:2 NCV) yet failed to find rest, I felt unloved. Or when I prayed nonstop yet missed "the peace of God, which transcends all understanding" (Philippians 4:7 NIV), I was broken.

One day I had a brutal awakening. In the worst of my distress, prayer often did me more harm than good. Why? Because my conversations with God amounted to little more than grinding on my problems. When I failed to connect with God, all I perceived was condemnation and even hatred. While God invites us to pour out our pain and plead our case with him, there are more ways we need to speak to God when we hurt.

I've written elsewhere that most people pray. Many of us struggle. We wonder what to say and how to say it. We worry if we will get what we ask or if we can speak honest questions. I created the *Pray the Scriptures Bible* to show how all of God's Word teaches us to pray. I wrote *Pray the Scriptures: A 40-Day Prayer Experience* to help people develop their own one-on-one conversation with God. *Pray the Scriptures When Life Hurts* helps us talk to God in our pain.

If one of the most practical reasons we pray is to obtain strength from God, then we need a thorough understanding of how that happens. Prayer is about more than making requests. Scripture teaches us to offer up not only our agony and questioning but also our surrender. We can voice not only loneliness, resentment, and frustration but also peace, hope, and worship. When we allow Scripture to lead us to a breadth of prayers, we begin to be filled with God's fresh life.

In this book I walk through nine key Scripture passages. For each I provide an opening thought, then split up the passage and offer words and short phrases to prompt you to pray Scripture back to God. You can follow these prompts—or cross them out and respond with your own thoughts. This isn't the time for pretty prayers. Talk straight with God. Tell him what you really think and feel. At the end of each chapter come questions to answer on your own or with others. Work through the book at your own pace. There's no rush to this process.

Your own pain might be large or small, inward or outward, public or private, chronic or acute. Wherever your life hurts right now, I pray that this book will help you hope again in God, finding perspective and healing as you pray all of the thoughts and emotions expressed in God's Word. I join the apostle Paul in this ancient prayer:

I fall to my knees and pray to the Father, the Creator of everything in heaven and on earth. I pray that from his glorious, unlimited resources he will empower you with inner strength through his Spirit. Then Christ will make his home in your hearts as you trust in him. Your roots will grow down into God's love and keep you strong. And may you have the power to understand, as all God's people should, how wide, how long, how high, and how deep his love is. May you experience the love of Christ, though it is too great to understand fully. Then you will be made complete with all the fullness of life and power that comes from God.

Ephesians 3:14–19 NLT

2

agony

My God, my God, why have you forsaken me? Why are you so far from saving me, so far from my cries of anguish? My God, I cry out by day, but you do not answer, by night, but I find no rest.

Psalm 22:1–2 NIV

I've hung around this world long enough that I assume I'm halfway to dead. And I accept the fact that I will encounter more suffering along the rest of my journey. Pain is inescapable. It gets personal. As human beings, there's no end to the variety of evil that invades our lives. As I watch our world, the list keeps getting longer and longer. Just for starters, we endure

- illness, accidents, aging, death
- premature births, handicaps, autism, Alzheimer's
- addictions, mental illness

- broken friendships, family conflict, marital discord, divorce
- mean people on the playground and in the classroom, cubicle, and corner office
- emotional, mental, physical, sexual abuse
- unemployment, underemployment, underwater mortgages
- spiritual confusion, intolerance, religious violence
- recession, terrorism, war, natural disasters, pandemics
- hunger, racism, homelessness, displaced refugees, and genocide

We can be certain of this: Because of the variety of evil and suffering in the world, there are people all around us in all kinds of agonizing physical, emotional, psychological, spiritual, and relational pain. Often we ourselves are those hurting people.

Presence

Some who endure pain sense God's presence. Whether they are well-known or ordinary people, we love to hear their stories. But I suspect that many of us hit by the worst of the worst wonder where God has gone. We expect his help but can't see it. We pour out our thoughts and emotions but get silence in return. Our agony often mixes with astonishment and anger at feeling abandoned.

A friend describes Nordic skiing in Colorado's vast Rocky Mountains with words borrowed from the classic film *Chariots of Fire*. Just as the Olympic sprinter Eric Liddell sensed God's approval as he bolted down a track, my friend feels God's pleasure as he glides silently across miles of crystalline snow.

At the deepest of my depression a completely different thought continually ran through my head. I sensed what I interpreted as God's scowl, even after I owned up to my failings and did my best to receive God's forgiveness. I often said to Lyn, "Tell me I'm an okay person." Instead of experiencing God coming near to me, if I saw God at all, it was across an ever-widening chasm. My agony was unbearable.

I'm not alone. The Bible is full of laments, loud expressions of personal pain and perceived distance from God. These outcries peak in the psalms. Psalm 22 records the hurt felt by the Old Testament's King David. His words so capture the depths of human agony that Jesus spoke them from the cross. The Lord quoted the psalm's opening words (see also Matthew 27:46). Other parts of the psalm precisely detail much of what Jesus endured during his crucifixion. He was ridiculed (Matthew 27:27–31, 39–44). Thirst caused his tongue to cling to his jaw (John 19:28). His hands and feet were pierced (John 20:25). Soldiers cast lots for his clothing (Matthew 27:35).

On the cross Jesus twisted in unimaginable pain, arms outstretched, suffering not only physical trauma but the weight of carrying the world's sins. He was cut off from the Father for our sake. He cried, "My God, my God, why have you forsaken me?" (Matthew 27:46). These facts assure us that God understands our pain. They also tell us that he's unafraid of our feelings. He can handle our outbursts, because when he walked in our hurt-filled world, he did anything but hide his sorrow.

Near

Our agony is real. Our perception that God has abandoned us is not. He fully grasps what we are going through and vows to never forsake us (Hebrews 13:5).

If the sorrow of Jesus the Son of God suffering on the cross feels too epic to compare to our own, we should still identify with David. A shrewd and mighty warrior, he stands as Israel's most beloved king. But the Bible repeatedly portrays him as a human being like the rest of us. His strengths—and failings—fill its pages. The words of Psalm 22 are first and forever his.

This song heading says that David set his lyrics to the tune "The Doe of the Morning" but doesn't specify the occasion. Whatever the situation, David's anguish left him feeling deserted. He looked back in Israel's history and saw that faithful people who went before him had trusted God and were not disappointed. But his pain made him feel worthless. His confidence in the Lord was resoundingly mocked. Nevertheless, he sought the presence of the God who had been with him since birth, "for trouble is near and there is no one to help." David finds peace as he reminds himself that God has been worth trusting all along. Agony brings an opportunity to affirm faith in God. And in the end David concludes that God has neither hidden his face nor failed to hear his cry. He shouts that "dominion belongs to the Lord and he rules over the nations."

PSALM 22:1–2

My God, my God, why have you forsaken me?
Why are you so far from saving me,
so far from my cries of anguish?
My God, I cry out by day, but you do not answer,
by night, but I find no rest.

God, where have you gone? You . . .

My pain . . .

PSALM 22:3–5

> Yet you are enthroned as the Holy One;
>   you are the one Israel praises.
> In you our ancestors put their trust;
>   they trusted and you delivered them.
> To you they cried out and were saved;
>   in you they trusted and were not put to shame.

Despite my feelings you are . . .

I trust you because . . .

PSALM 22:6–8

But I am a worm and not a man,
 scorned by everyone, despised by the people.
All who see me mock me;
 they hurl insults, shaking their heads.
"He trusts in the Lord," they say,
 "let the Lord rescue him.
Let him deliver him,
 since he delights in him."

I barely feel human. I . . .

People mock me . . .

PSALM 22:9–11

Yet you brought me out of the womb;
> you made me trust in you, even at my mother's
>> breast.

From birth I was cast on you;
> from my mother's womb you have been my God.

Do not be far from me,
> for trouble is near
> and there is no one to help.

Because you have been with me from my birth . . .

Because you are my God . . .

PSALM 22:12–18

Many bulls surround me;
   strong bulls of Bashan[1] encircle me.
Roaring lions that tear their prey
   open their mouths wide against me.
I am poured out like water,
   and all my bones are out of joint.
My heart has turned to wax;
   it has melted within me.
My mouth is dried up like a potsherd,
   and my tongue sticks to the roof of my mouth;
   you lay me in the dust of death.
Dogs surround me,
   a pack of villains encircles me;
   they pierce my hands and my feet.
All my bones are on display;
   people stare and gloat over me.
They divide my clothes among them
   and cast lots for my garment.

I'm surrounded by . . .

My strength . . .

I can't take any more . . .

---

1. Bashan was a rich and fertile territory east of the Jordan River. It symbolizes selfishness and arrogance.

Psalm 22:19–21

But you, Lord, do not be far from me.
    You are my strength; come quickly to help me.
Deliver me from the sword,
    my precious life from the power of the dogs.
Rescue me from the mouth of the lions;
    save me from the horns of the wild oxen.

I need you to . . .

If you don't rescue me, I fear . . .

PSALM 22:22–24

> I will declare your name to my people;
>> in the assembly I will praise you.
> You who fear the Lord, praise him!
>> All you descendants of Jacob,[2] honor him!
>> Revere him, all you descendants of Israel!
> For he has not despised or scorned
>> the suffering of the afflicted one;
> he has not hidden his face from him
>> but has listened to his cry for help.

I will share your faithfulness with . . .

I will tell them . . .

2. Jacob was a significant patriarch of God's people. God gave him a new name, Israel (Genesis 35:10).

Reflect + Pray + Discuss

1. In what areas of life have you suffered most? What hurts do you face right now?

2. When has pain made you feel closer to God? When has your agony caused you to feel abandoned?

3. What steps can you take to close any gap that you feel between yourself and God?

3

loneliness

[Elijah] answered, "Lord God of Armies, I have eagerly served you. The Israelites have abandoned your promises, torn down your altars, and executed your prophets. I'm the only one left, and they're trying to take my life."

1 Kings 19:10 GOD'S WORD

A while back I attended a gathering of several dozen youth workers, reconnecting with a world I missed since I became a solo pastor of a small church. I saw an old friend who pops into my life unexpectedly, as if to make sure I'm okay. I spent time with a leader I knew from a distance but had never met in person. I enjoyed an hour with a guy I've wanted to meet for ten years, ever since a mutual friend said we needed to connect. And I joined a spontaneous group that sprung up to discuss the topic "I didn't know ministry would be this hard."

Into this setting wandered someone I hadn't talked to in years—an old friend—almost an ex-friend. We had worked together on a major project that fell apart. After that setback I never knew what to say. I wanted to move on. But there this person was, ten feet behind me. I made the first move. I walked over. We talked.

When life hurts, we often cut ourselves off from the world. We make excuses so we don't have to face old friends. We avoid situations where we're forced to mix. During the worst waves of my depression and illnesses, I let few people in. Some I didn't trust. Others I didn't want to bother. With inadequate justification, I decided that few understood me. Ironically, people are often the source of our hurt, but they're also essential to our wholeness. Pain can cause devastating loneliness, but putting ourselves in the midst of friends can heal us.

Alone

Rough clothing and a shaggy appearance earned the Old Testament prophet Elijah the name "the hairy guy" (see 2 Kings 1:8). This spiritual wild man camped in caves. Birds brought him meals of bread and meat. No one could accuse Elijah of weakness. But no one could miss his array of painful relationships.

God sent this prophet to confront King Ahab and Queen Jezebel, Israel's vile and dangerous rulers. They had set up idols, murdered God's representatives, and incited the nation to brazen injustice and immorality. Elijah walked into their royal court and declared that no rain would fall until he requested it from God (1 Kings 17:1). Three bone-dry years later, God told Elijah to pick another fight. The prophet summoned hundreds of pagan prophets to a mountaintop showdown. He called down fire from heaven, defeated his opponents, and demonstrated that he spoke for God (1 Kings 18:1–46).

That bloody mountaintop scene shows how mayhem results when people turn against God and each other. Afterward, not much changed. When Queen Jezebel vowed to kill Elijah, he fled as fast and as far as he could, running almost a hundred miles southward until he ended up completely alone.

Done

Elijah collapsed under a large shrub and informed God he was giving up. He felt misunderstood, shut out, persecuted. He didn't just say, "God, I want to die." He wanted God to hasten the end. He pleaded, "God, put me out of my misery. Kill me here and now." Then he rolled over and fell asleep.

Our own eyes well up at the challenges we face. Our inner hurts shut us down. But God's tender and practical response to Elijah points us to a better place.

As Elijah hid amid rocks and desert sand, God served up hot bread and fresh water. Refreshed, the prophet walked forty days and nights until he reached the mountain of God, where he entered a cave and again slept. Countless times I've said to Lyn, "I want to crawl in a hole." Elijah actually did.

When Elijah awoke, God spoke. He had one question. "Elijah, what are you doing here?" As in—Elijah, what do you want? Elijah, what do you need? Elijah, why did you come all this way?

The prophet answered, "Lord God of Armies, I have eagerly served you. The Israelites have abandoned your promises, torn down your altars, and executed your prophets. I'm the only one left, and they're trying to take my life." Elijah felt crushed and alone. He seemed to think his plight was God's fault.

Elijah stood on God's mountain, waiting for God. The Lord didn't show up in wind. Or an earthquake. Or fire. God instead approached Elijah in "a gentle whisper," what the King James

Version of the Bible famously calls a "still small voice." Again God asked, "Elijah, what are you doing here?"

The repeated question implies that there was now somewhere else the prophet should be. The Lord had put his glory on display. But remaining on God's mountain wasn't enough to address Elijah's need for relationship. God's presence alone can't solve our problem of feeling alone.

Elijah was isolated, in part by his own choice. So God sent him homeward to friends who could help him. The Lord gave him a defender, Hazael. He provided a ministry partner, Elisha. And he surrounded Elijah with a faithful community, thousands who bowed only to God.

When life hurts, little does us more harm than disconnecting from the people God sends to lift us up. Our daily job is to seek them out, even when it means a long walk back.

1 KINGS 19:1–2

Ahab told Jezebel everything Elijah had done, including how he had executed all the prophets. Then Jezebel sent a messenger to Elijah. She said, "May the gods strike me dead if by this time tomorrow I don't take your life the way you took the lives of Baal's prophets."

People think I . . .

My adversaries make me feel . . .

People threaten to . . .

1 KINGS 19:3–5

Frightened, Elijah fled to save his life. He came to Beer-sheba in Judah and left his servant there. Then he traveled through the wilderness for a day. He sat down under a broom plant and wanted to die. "I've had enough now, Lord," he said. "Take my life! I'm no better than my ancestors." Then he lay down and slept under the broom plant.

I'm frightened when . . .

I'm running away from . . .

1 KINGS 19:5–9

An angel touched him and said, "Get up and eat." When he looked, he saw near his head some bread baked on hot stones and a jar of water. So he ate, drank, and went to sleep again.

The angel of the Lord came back and woke him up again. The angel said, "Get up and eat, or your journey will be too much for you."

He got up, ate, and drank. Strengthened by that food, he traveled for 40 days and nights until he came to Horeb, the mountain of God. There he went into a cave and spent the night.

I need your practical comfort. Please . . .

Give me strength for . . .

1 Kings 19:9–10

Then the Lord spoke his word to Elijah. He asked, "What are you doing here, Elijah?"

He answered, "Lord God of Armies, I have eagerly served you. The Israelites have abandoned your promises, torn down your altars, and executed your prophets. I'm the only one left, and they're trying to take my life."

I've come to you because . . .

People have failed me by . . .

I feel distant from . . .

1 KINGS 19:11–13

God said, "Go out and stand in front of the Lord on the mountain." As the Lord was passing by, a fierce wind tore mountains and shattered rocks ahead of the Lord. But the Lord was not in the wind. After the wind came an earthquake. But the Lord wasn't in the earthquake. After the earthquake there was a fire. But the Lord wasn't in the fire. And after the fire there was a quiet, whispering voice. When Elijah heard it, he wrapped his face in his coat, went out, and stood at the entrance of the cave.

Show me yourself by . . .

I'm waiting for you to . . .

1 KINGS 19:13–18

Then the voice said to him, "What are you doing here, Elijah?"

He answered, "Lord God of Armies, I have eagerly served you. The Israelites have abandoned your promises, torn down your altars, and executed your prophets. I'm the only one left, and they're trying to take my life."

The Lord told him, "Go back to the wilderness near Damascus, the same way you came. When you get there, anoint Hazael as king of Aram. Anoint Jehu, son of Nimshi, as king of Israel. And anoint Elisha, son of Shaphat, from Abel Meholah as prophet to take your place. If anyone escapes from Hazael's sword, Jehu will kill him. And if anyone escapes from Jehu's sword, Elisha will kill him. But I still have 7,000 people in Israel whose knees have not knelt to worship Baal and whose mouths have not kissed him."

I still feel alone because . . .

I need people who . . .

I need your help overcoming obstacles such as . . .

Reflect + Pray + Discuss

1. Who has caused you deep hurt? How are you addressing that?

2. Who in your world understands your suffering? In what specific ways can you rely on that person?

3. What help do you expect God alone to provide? What help do you need from his people?

4

questions

> If I have sinned, what have I done to you, you watcher
> of humans? Why have you made me your target?
> Have I become a heavy load for you? Why don't you
> pardon my wrongs and forgive my sins?
>
> Job 7:20–21 NCV

The Old Testament character Job (rhymes with "robe") was fantastically well-off. He was dubbed "the greatest man among all the people of the East" (Job 1:3). No one would have blamed this leading influencer for taking credit for his wealth and fame. But he knew that God had made him the biggest man around.

While Job savored life's pleasantness, an unseen drama unfolded in heaven. Satan and the Lord debated Job's integrity. The evil one argued that Job only obeyed God and did good because of the phenomenal blessings the Lord had bestowed. When Satan insisted on testing Job's faithfulness, God gave his consent. Job was hit with multiple disasters. Raiders made off with thousands of animals. Fire consumed thousands more. His servants met violent deaths. A fierce wind killed all ten of his children.

Job grieved. He tore his clothes and shaved his head. But he nevertheless fell to the ground in worship. "The Lord gave me what I had," he acknowledged, "and the Lord has taken it away. Praise the name of the Lord!" (Job 1:21 NLT).

In a final test of Job's faithfulness, excruciating sores covered his body. The financially destitute and physically broken man sat atop a heap of ashes, scraping his oozing skin with a shard of broken pottery. Job's wife wandered by and told him to curse God and die, yet Job refused to say anything bad about the Lord (Job 1:6–10). Job grieved silently for seven days. When he finally spoke, he wished he had never been born (Job 2:11–3:26). His mouth exploded with protests and questions.

Firsts

Some of the deepest anguish I ever see shows itself in people experiencing painful "firsts." They feel shock when a relationship fails. Or an illness can't be cured. Or a problem won't go away. Their pain multiplies if they are the first among their family and friends to face a particular difficulty. They discover that some people brush off their struggles. Others back away, unsure how to help.

Honestly, we're often startled when suffering intrudes on our lives. We might not like to admit it, but we count on God for health, wealth, and happiness. When we picture a life blessed by God, doesn't it include protection from all kinds of harm? Don't we expect financial success, even if it's something other than thousands of sheep and camels in our backyard? Don't we expect our children to turn out well? Doesn't our dream include accumulating enough to retire to a lake or beach or hip urban condo? But things happen beyond our control. Bodies break. Loved ones die. People flake out. Storms hit. Wars start. Businesses downsize. Our problems start to feel unsolvable. There's a disconnect between the pain we experience and the life we expect God to grant us if we just walk close to him. We thrive when God gives. We struggle when he takes away.

I know that when I hurt, resignation isn't an option. I don't roll over and take it. Every part of me rises up. I fight back. And I can usually cope as long as I think relief is on its way. I might tell myself, "God won't give me more than I can handle," but that only works until I get more than I can take. Or I might think, "God will bring something good out of this," but that hope lies so far in the future that it feels beyond reach. Or I might console myself that "God will protect me from the worst of the worst," but then the frequency, intensity, and duration of pain becomes more unrelenting than I ever expect.

Questions

That's when the tough questions really begin. We ask them of ourselves, our friends, anyone we think is wise. We hurl them at God, who by definition sees all and understands all. He surely has the answers we crave:

- Why does my pain go on and on?
- Why doesn't God heal?
- Why won't he lead me to a better place?
- Why can't he show the care I show others?
- Whom can I count on?
- What about those friends God promised?
- Where is his fullness of life?

43

- Why don't I see God's miraculous provision?
- Why doesn't he put a stop to evil?
- What is the purpose of all this?

We ask, "What?" *God—what is going on?* We wonder, "Why?" *God—why is this happening?* We plead, "Who?" *God—who are you?*

Jesus said, "Here on earth you will have many trials and sorrows" (John 16:33 NLT). But Jesus refused to offer a simplistic response to our deep questions. No single answer fully explains why we suffer. The whole of the Bible shows that sometimes *we bring pain on ourselves.* We ignore God's directions for life, and we end up in unhappy places. We slam our hand in the car door of life and wonder why it hurts or how God could do such a thing. But responsibility is ours. Or we might suffer because *we are on the receiving end of other people's wrongdoing.* Families and organizations are sick. Societies and governments engage in systemic evil. Everyone sins and everyone suffers for it. And sometimes we experience pain because *we live in a broken world.* This is the Bible's explanation for unexplainable things. Human wrongdoing has so shattered our world that the natural order is riddled with disaster and disease (Romans 8:20–22).

Answers

When our hearts and minds overflow with questions, Jesus offers the ultimate answer: He overcomes our troubles (John 16:33). As we wait for that to work out, God welcomes our questions. Read the entire book of Job, and you'll see God let this suffering man and his friends talk until they ran out of breath. Only then does he assert his wisdom and power. We can be sure that God can handle our pain-filled wonderings, whether angry shouts or weeping whispers. And at some point we can start to ask better questions. I learned to stop asking, "Where is God?" I instead asked, "Where is God in this?" Rather than asking, "Why am I suffering?" I began to wonder "What now?" "How do I deal with this?" "How do I move forward?" These are questions God seems eager to answer.

Job 7:1–2

> "People have a hard task on earth,
>   and their days are like those of a laborer.
> They are like a slave wishing for the evening
>   shadows,
>   like a laborer waiting to be paid."

My days are . . .

I find myself wishing . . .

Job 7:3–4

"But I am given months that are empty,
and nights of misery have been given to me.
When I lie down, I think, 'How long until I get up?'
The night is long, and I toss until dawn."

My suffering has gone on for . . .

My pain comes out in . . .

Job 7:5–7

"My body is covered with worms and scabs,
   and my skin is broken and full of sores.
My days go by faster than a weaver's tool,
   and they come to an end without hope.
Remember, God, that my life is only a breath.
   My eyes will never see happy times again."

My body feels . . .

I worry that . . .

JOB 7:8–10

"Those who see me now will see me no more;
  you will look for me, but I will be gone.
As a cloud disappears and is gone,
  people go to the grave and never return.
They will never come back to their houses again,
  and their places will not know them anymore."

The future looks . . .

I fear that . . .

JOB 7:11–12

> "So I will not stay quiet;
>> I will speak out in the suffering of my spirit.
>> I will complain because I am so unhappy.
> I am not the sea or the sea monster.[1]
>> So why have you set a guard over me?"

I will . . .

I won't . . .

1. The "sea" and the "sea monster" both embodied chaos. Some ancient religions considered them gods.

JOB 7:13–15

> "Sometimes I think my bed will comfort me
>   or that my couch will stop my complaint.
> Then you frighten me with dreams
>   and terrify me with visions.
> My throat prefers to be choked;
>   my bones welcome death."

At night I . . .

My dreams . . .

Job 7:16–19

"I hate my life; I don't want to live forever.
  Leave me alone, because my days have no
    meaning.
Why do you make people so important
  and give them so much attention?
You examine them every morning
  and test them every moment.
Will you never look away from me
  or leave me alone even long enough to swallow?"

I hate . . .

You . . .

JOB 7:20–21

"If I have sinned, what have I done to you,
    you watcher of humans?
Why have you made me your target?
    Have I become a heavy load for you?
Why don't you pardon my wrongs
    and forgive my sins?
I will soon lie down in the dust of death.
    Then you will search for me, but I will be no
        more."

Why can't you . . .

When will you . . .

Reflect + Pray + Discuss

1. What are your most troubling questions you wish God would answer?

2. Who can you trust to hear your questions and help you find answers?

3. What will you do if some of your questions never get a full answer?

5

resentment

But I had almost stopped believing; I had almost lost
my faith because I was jealous of proud people. I
saw wicked people doing well.

Psalm 73:2–3 NCV

On my last morning of work the summer before I started college,
police officer James Anderson responded to a domestic distur-
bance a few blocks from my workplace in suburban Minneapolis.
As he entered a small apartment building, an enraged young man
shot and killed him. The suspect fled to city hall, where he shot
two more people. A third person was injured diving through a
window to escape. Another officer was wounded by shrapnel.
At a nearby post office the shooter took nine hostages, begin-
ning a standoff that lasted until late afternoon, when he freed
his captives and took his own life.

The little house where I worked as a lab technician sat in a direct path of the unfolding events. City hall was across the street. Our wide back window looked across an empty lot to the post office. For much of the day we knew nothing more than that a gunman was loose. We checked the locks. We cleared the creepy basement. We waited for an armed killer to pound on the door. After several uneasy hours, we discovered we had been overlooked in an evacuation. When we were finally led to safety, we saw some of the hundred-plus police who had swarmed the area along with four SWAT teams. When officers led us past barricades, I kept walking. My car was stranded back inside, and I needed to call home.

Within a couple minutes I was at a payphone in an ice cream shop. I felt a jolt of disbelief as I watched customers talk and laugh and order treats. I dialed home and reached my mom and shouted, "I'm okay!"

"What do you mean you're okay? What's wrong?"

I assumed everyone knew about the shootings and standoff. But the world seemed oblivious to the nearby trauma, injury, and death.

Envy

When we endure any kind of hurt, it's shocking to watch the rest of the world go on with life as usual. They don't understand our pain. Or seem to not see it. Or choose to ignore it. We feel slighted, discounted, forgotten. The more we brood over the situation, the more confounded we feel. Why has our life gone wrong? Why is theirs so much easier, better, more abundant? They feel good. We feel ghastly. They get ahead. We fall behind. They get by on good luck. We get thumped by all kinds of misfortune. We notice that some do wrong and get away with it. We do good and have little to show for it. On top of whatever outward trouble we're dealing with, we might contend with an inner envy toward others. You might begin to resent

- the slacker who beats you out for the promotion
- the woman who survives cancer when you're still at risk
- the friend who loudly criticizes you for her own obvious failings
- the classmate who cheats his way to the top of the class
- the spouse who refuses to meet your needs
- the son or daughter who does nothing to help
- the relative who accumulates piles of money while you struggle
- the neighbor whose life is all put together while yours falls apart

Nothing seems fair. Injustice rules. Our anger, bitterness, and resentment boil over.

Reality

The Old Testament songwriter Asaph understood those feelings. He had every reason to be happy. He was among those whose job it was to strum harps, clang cymbals, and sing joyous songs (1 Chronicles 15:16–19). And yet Asaph admits to being confused by the unfairness of life. He calls himself sad, angry, senseless, and stupid. Psalm 73 captures Asaph's conversation as he thinks out loud with God.

Asaph's problem began when he observed wicked people flourish. They never suffer. Their bodies stand strong. They dodge the problems that overwhelm normal people. Their success breeds arrogance, so that they "wear pride like a necklace and put on violence as their clothing." They exploit others for profit, live by a code of selfishness, mock those who struggle, and brag about their ability to inflict pain. They believe that God winks at their evil ways.

Asaph admits that his jealousy nearly killed his faith in God. After all, he had kept his heart pure. He refused to do wrong. He put up with endless pain. He got up day after day to fresh punishment. Why bother being good and obeying God? Why trust? Why not act like an animal?

Then Asaph realizes two things. First, if people persistently do wrong, God puts them in a precarious position. Asaph doesn't need to carry the burden of injustice, because God will take care of that. We can let go of our own resentment knowing that if we suffer real offenses—if they are more than a figment of our embittered imaginations—God will deal with those who harm us.

Second, Asaph possesses something that outweighs all his losses. His intimacy with God is an experience we too are meant to enjoy. "I am always with you," he prays. "You have held my hand. You guide me with your advice, and later you will receive me in honor. I have no one in heaven but you. I want nothing on earth besides you. My body and my mind may become weak, but God is my strength. He is mine forever."

God takes you by the hand. He will never let go. When life falls apart, you still have everything you truly need. If you have God, that's enough.

PSALM 73:1–3

> God is truly good to Israel,
>   to those who have pure hearts.
> But I had almost stopped believing;
>   I had almost lost my faith
> because I was jealous of proud people.
>   I saw wicked people doing well.

God, you are . . .

Sometimes I have trouble believing in you because . . .

PSALM 73:4–10

They are not suffering;
    they are healthy and strong.
They don't have troubles like the rest of us;
    they don't have problems like other people.
They wear pride like a necklace
    and put on violence as their clothing.
They are looking for profits
    and do not control their selfish desires.
They make fun of others and speak evil;
    proudly they speak of hurting others.
They brag to the sky.
    They say that they own the earth.
So their people turn to them
    and give them whatever they want.

Some people have it all. They . . .

I see what they have and I feel . . .

PSALM 73:11–14

They say, "How can God know?
> What does God Most High know?"
These people are wicked,
> always at ease, and getting richer.
So why have I kept my heart pure?
> Why have I kept my hands from doing wrong?
I have suffered all day long;
> I have been punished every morning.

I wonder why I bother to . . .

I fear today will bring . . .

PSALM 73:15–20

God, if I had decided to talk like this,
    I would have let your people down.
I tried to understand all this,
    but it was too hard for me to see
until I went to the Temple of God.
    Then I understood what will happen to them.
You have put them in danger;
    you cause them to be destroyed.
They are destroyed in a moment;
    they are swept away by terrors.
It will be like waking from a dream.
    Lord, when you rise up, they will disappear.

Only you can make sense of . . .

I'm sure that . . .

PSALM 73:21–26

When my heart was sad
and I was angry,
I was senseless and stupid.
I acted like an animal toward you.
But I am always with you;
you have held my hand.
You guide me with your advice,
and later you will receive me in honor.
I have no one in heaven but you;
I want nothing on earth besides you.
My body and my mind may become weak,
but God is my strength.
He is mine forever.

You . . .

Because I have you, I . . .

PSALM 73:27–28

> Those who are far from God will die;
>   you destroy those who are unfaithful.
> But I am close to God, and that is good.
>   The Lord God is my protection.
>   I will tell all that you have done.

Having you near . . .

I will tell . . .

Reflect + Pray + Discuss

1. When have you felt your hurts downplayed or overlooked?

2. How do you react when others seem to have an easier life than you do?

3. How does Psalm 73 change how you think about the unfairness of life?

6

requests

[Jesus said,] "Ask and it will be given to you; seek and you will find; knock and the door will be opened to you. For everyone who asks receives; the one who seeks finds; and to the one who knocks, the door will be opened."

Luke 11:9–10 NIV

I inherited Kit and Luann as volunteers at a church where I pastored several hundred junior highers and their families. Luann had led students in a drama ministry for nearly twenty years. Every week without fail, her kids grabbed the attention of our little mob. Besides teaming up with Luann to do drama, Kit helped me lead worship, skillfully rocking the sound with an amazing assortment of guitars. He became my beloved mentor, a quiet older guy who let me spout off as I maneuvered my first adult job.

One week Kit had to cancel one of our frequent lunches. What he assumed was a fortysomething backache turned out to be cancer. His illness progressed quickly. I sang to my friend when he became too sick to play. I watched him stubbornly wobble down hospital halls as malignancies spread to his brain. I rushed back to the hospital and held his hand moments after he passed away. Hundreds of kids and adults witnessed Kit and Luann's struggle. Until the end we prayed for Kit's healing, asking for a yes until God said a definitive no. The situation forced our prayers deep. As Luann says, "I don't pray for parking spots anymore."

Simple

We might be perplexed by the Bible's oversized promises regarding prayer. Jesus says we'll get what we ask for. We'll find what we're looking for. Doors will swing open when we knock.

Jesus makes those promises in the middle of a longer teachable moment with his followers. They had caught him in prayer. When he was done, they said, "Lord, teach us to pray." Everyone knew that the religious leaders of the day thought prayers should be loud and long (Matthew 6:7; Luke 18:11–12). They spoke to God on street corners where everyone could see them (Matthew 6:5). But Jesus coached his friends to pray simply:

> "Father,
> hallowed be your name,
> your kingdom come.
> Give us each day our daily bread.
> Forgive us our sins,
>   for we also forgive everyone who sins against us.
> And lead us not into temptation."
>
> Luke 11:2–4

That prayer couldn't be more straightforward. It worships God. It invites his reign. It asks him to meet real needs day by day. It comes clean about wrongdoing and grants forgiveness to those who hurt us. And it presses for God's help avoiding the pitfalls of evil.

Jesus says, "Pray like that." Then he tells a story to encourage his followers to keep praying. It goes something like this: Suppose a guest shows up at your house in the wee hours of the night, exhausted after a long trip. You've got nothing to feed him, so you pound on a neighbor's door. Your neighbor doesn't want to get out of bed. He worries about waking his wife and their little ones—especially the baby, who stirs at the tiniest noise. Despite your neighbor's objections, however, your boldness gets you what you need.

Boldness

When life hurts, simple prayer is often exactly what we need, yet sometimes even the shortest and most straightforward words feel like more than we can manage. And what can really halt our prayers is fear that God is that reluctant neighbor on the other side of a locked door. He's slow to get up. He's unenthusiastic about granting our request. He puts up a legitimate fuss, especially given the ancient setting where families often slept in a single room with a creaky metal bolt securing the outside door. If we expect that irritable response from God, we shut down. Why pray if God doesn't want to be bothered?

But that isn't the gist of Jesus' story. The star of this parable isn't the cranky neighbor. Jesus never equates him with God. He doesn't picture a God unwilling to come to the door or imply that God needs to be pestered until he gives in. Jesus instead teaches us to speak up about our needs. He wants us to imitate the man who reaches out for help with "boldness" (NCV) or "impudence" (ESV) or "shameless audacity" (NIV).

69

It's at the moment when we hurt the most—right when we've tired of telling God what we need—that Jesus says, "Keep at it." The grammar underlying his words signals that we get what we need when we ask and keep asking. We find what we're looking for when we search and keep searching. Doors swing open when we knock and keep knocking.

As if to clear up any doubts about God's love for us, Jesus offers an outrageous illustration. He points out that no human parent would hear a child's request for a fish and hand him a snake. Or a request for an egg and give him a scorpion. If evil people manage to give their children good gifts, then God surely will do even better.

Words

Before I sunk into despair, I had never hesitated to go to God with any kind of ask. But how many ways could I say I was aching for sound sleep, quiet nerves, and a change in scenery? What part of my problems did I need to explain further? Was God tired of my complaints?

I ran out of words to say what I needed. But as I made a more conscious habit of praying the Scriptures, God gave me new words. Even when I hurt, he opened up a fresh conversation. I learned to follow his lead through all the things he wants to talk about. I felt reassured that he never tires of meeting my needs.

In time I also found that the topics of our conversations changed. Instead of my grinding on the same old issues, God shifted my focus. He answered requests I never spoke. He helped me find things I didn't know I was looking for. Doors swung open and caught me by surprise. My goal was a quick fix. God's intent is always to build bold trust. No matter what results we do or don't get, he aims to grow a relationship based on belief in his unwavering care.

LUKE 11:5–6

Then Jesus said to them, "Suppose you have a friend, and you go to him at midnight and say, 'Friend, lend me three loaves of bread; a friend of mine on a journey has come to me, and I have no food to offer him.'"

I'm in a jam. I need . . .

No one but you can . . .

Luke 11:7–8

"And suppose the one inside answers, 'Don't bother me. The door is already locked, and my children and I are in bed. I can't get up and give you anything.' I tell you, even though he will not get up and give you the bread because of friendship, yet because of your shameless audacity he will surely get up and give you as much as you need."

I give up on you when . . .

I trust you not to turn me away. You . . .

Teach me to boldly . . .

Luke 11:9–10

"So I say to you: Ask and it will be given to you; seek and you will find; knock and the door will be opened to you. For everyone who asks receives; the one who seeks finds; and to the one who knocks, the door will be opened."

I've made up my mind to . . .

Teach me persistence when . . .

LUKE 11:11–13

"Which of you fathers, if your son asks for a fish, will give him a snake instead? Or if he asks for an egg, will give him a scorpion? If you then, though you are evil, know how to give good gifts to your children, how much more will your Father in heaven give the Holy Spirit to those who ask him!"

You would never . . .

You give me . . .

I'm grateful for . . .

Reflect + Pray + Discuss

1. Do you expect God to respond to your requests? Why—or why not?

2. Have you ever run out of words to pray or given up on prayer altogether? When? Why?

3. What keeps you from telling God your needs right now?

7

frustration

> I was given a thorn in my flesh, a messenger from
> Satan to torment me and keep me from becoming
> proud. Three different times I begged the Lord to
> take it away. Each time he said, "My grace is all you
> need. My power works best in weakness."
>
> 2 Corinthians 12:7–9 NLT

Five years after a neurologist diagnosed why my body feels like
it's plugged into an electrical outlet, the sensation still comes in
waves, never completely subsiding. My little muscles constantly
twitch. Big ones thump off and on. If I pay attention, there are
always three or four buzzes and bumps going on somewhere
in my body. Because my symptoms are nothing more than an
annoyance, I ignore the chaos.

But a year ago the buzzing spread from my legs to my stom-
ach and chest to create a loud, nauseating hum inside. A new

neurologist assured me that my symptoms were more of the same—nothing grave—and prescribed the most promising option, a potent antiseizure medication. Popping a dozen capsules a day gave significant relief. But it also brought a side effect everyone calls "the drunken sailor." I felt tipsy. I moved cautiously. Walls became my friends, something to hang on to just in case. After pushing the dosage to my limit, I decided to slowly taper off the meds.

Pleading

I'm back to trying to ignore my symptoms. Honestly, at times I wish I could escape my body or at least detach my legs until they quiet down. I've uttered no shortage of prayers pleading for relief, but the problem persists.

I can't help but feel sympathy for the apostle Paul, who prayed repeatedly for God to take away what he called "a thorn in my flesh." No one can say for sure, but that thorn might have been a debilitating eye problem. Or some dire malady. It could have been Paul's conflicts with violent opponents. Or something else altogether.

Whatever it was, Paul's thorn sounds like our own persistent hurts. Whether major or minor, public or private, chronic or acute, they cause us to cry desperately for relief, yet God seems to refuse our requests. It would be easier if God always gave us what we want—or if he never did. As it is, we struggle to make sense of his answers. We wonder why he lets our pain continue.

Despite repeated pleading, Paul's thorn remained. God triple-vetoed Paul's request. Why? Sometimes we don't get what we want because we don't ask (James 4:2). Sometimes we ask selfishly (v. 3). Sometimes our requests don't line up with God's will (1 John 5:14). Sometimes the reasons God says yes or no are simply beyond our grasp. But in this case he offered Paul a specific explanation for his ongoing affliction. The thorn brought Paul low. In Paul's weakness, God's strength would be obvious.

Paul experienced God's power and presence in ways beyond our imagination. He describes being caught up to paradise, where he "heard things so astounding that they cannot be expressed in words, things no human is allowed to tell." When his opponents challenged his spiritual credentials, he could have bragged about this up-close encounter. But he didn't. He instead pointed to his weakness.

Paul got a hard dose of humility. I wish I knew the rest of his story. What was his thorn? Was he constantly miserable? How did he cope day by day? For all we know, Paul lived with that stabbing pain for the rest of his life. Yet he reached the point where he was glad to be weak so that Christ's power could be displayed in him. "That's why I take pleasure in my weaknesses," he said, "and in the insults, hardships, persecutions, and troubles that I suffer for Christ. For when I am weak, then I am strong." Whatever challenges Paul faced, he clung to God's promise that "My grace is all you need. My power works best in weakness." When our own hurts are unending, we too can be sure that God has grace for us.

Message

The need to learn humility isn't a one-size-fits-all explanation for pain that won't go away. I also hesitate to tell hurting people that "God has something to teach you," because I know firsthand that it feels dismissive of personal pain. What God might want to teach us is a conclusion we usually need to reach on our own. But I also know that finding grace in the midst of weakness is always part of God's plan.

At the point when I felt completely broken, I had a long list of things I wanted from God. Who doesn't? But after hearing one no from God after another, I got the message that I was *asking* him to do things for me when I instead needed to *act*.

For years I pleaded with God to throw open a door to an authentic community where I could thrive. That eventually happened. But I got something else along the way—a more thorough understanding of who I am, where I fit, and what I'm wired to do. A counselor who put me through a rigorous psychological assessment said I had all the makings of an evil genius if I weren't so hopelessly committed to the good of others. I make my mark through intellect and nonconformity, but I'm also big on empathy, tolerance, and altruism. I'm inwardly driven to do the right thing, so at times I'm exceedingly hard on myself. What does that add up to? I need to partner with kindhearted people on a genuine mission where creativity is an asset.

At my worst I also thought I knew what was best for my life. I knew exactly how God should answer my prayers and make everything fall in place. But God signed me up for a different program. When I asked him to fix my body, he told me to take charge of my health. When I told him I needed help with my sleep, he pointed out ways I contribute to my insomnia. When I prayed for relief from mental anguish, he forced me to ask for real human help from my doctor, my family, and a handful of good listeners who patiently heard my woes and led me back to real life.

Like I've said, God has answered requests I never spoke. He helped me find things I didn't know I was looking for. Doors swung open and caught me by surprise. Even when God says a loud no to our requests, his grace comes to us, often in ways we never expect.

2 CORINTHIANS 12:1–4

This boasting will do no good, but I must go on. I will reluctantly tell about visions and revelations from the Lord. I was caught up to the third heaven fourteen years ago. Whether I was in my body or out of my body, I don't know—only God knows. Yes, only God knows whether I was in my body or outside my body. But I do know that I was caught up to paradise and heard things so astounding that they cannot be expressed in words, things no human is allowed to tell.

In the past you've shown yourself to me by . . .

Now I see you . . .

2 CORINTHIANS 12:5–7

That experience is worth boasting about, but I'm not going to do it. I will boast only about my weaknesses. If I wanted to boast, I would be no fool in doing so, because I would be telling the truth. But I won't do it, because I don't want anyone to give me credit beyond what they can see in my life or hear in my message, even though I have received such wonderful revelations from God.

I'm weak . . .

I give you credit for . . .

2 CORINTHIANS 12:7

So to keep me from becoming proud, I was given a thorn in my flesh, a messenger from Satan to torment me and keep me from becoming proud.

I'm still suffering . . .

I don't understand . . .

2 CORINTHIANS 12:8

Three different times I begged the Lord to take it away.

You've said no to . . .

When you say no to my pleading I feel . . .

2 CORINTHIANS 12:9–10

Each time he said, "My grace is all you need. My power works best in weakness." So now I am glad to boast about my weaknesses, so that the power of Christ can work through me. That's why I take pleasure in my weaknesses, and in the insults, hardships, persecutions, and troubles that I suffer for Christ. For when I am weak, then I am strong.

I think you're telling me . . .

I choose to accept . . .

I need your grace . . .

Reflect + Pray + Discuss

1. When has God said no to your urgent request?

2. What sense can you make of his response?

3. What practical steps will you take to press on?

8

peace

Do not be anxious about anything, but in every situation, by prayer and petition, with thanksgiving, present your requests to God. And the peace of God, which transcends all understanding, will guard your hearts and your minds in Christ Jesus.

Philippians 4:6–7 NIV

Finding out in my forties about my crazy nerves, noxious liver, and cantankerous gallbladder wasn't my first close encounter with doctors. Years earlier I had lain on my back under blazing operating room lights, being prepped for an angiogram, a test healthy guys in their twenties don't undergo unless they have crushing chest pains coupled with a family history that includes an uncle who had his first heart attack at thirty-two and another who died of a stroke at thirty-seven. With no warning, I called the church and put my rookie intern in charge of leading dozens of eighth graders on a 140-mile bike trek across Wisconsin's rolling hills so a cardiologist could thread a camera into my thigh and up to my heart.

For months before that moment, doctors had scrutinized everything between my nose and my belly button to diagnose my pain. Each time a test came back negative, people around me said, "So you're okay! Great!" I thought, "No! I'm not okay. I still hurt. My doctors don't know what's wrong. I still might die!" Unfortunately, I was also dealing with a hole in the retina of my right eye that was causing a bubbling partial detachment. I was doubly angry: "No! I am NOT okay. I might go BLIND. I might DIE!"

Anxious

Eventually my eye healed, other than a small blotch in my vision that my brain usually ignores. And while I was still on the operating table, my cardiologist declared that my arteries were "clear enough to drive a truck through," which sounded plenty good. I had a few more tests to rule out other issues, and after a while my puzzled doctors sent me on my way.

I've concluded that my pain comes from spasms in my esophagus, a theory doctors can't confirm unless it happens when they have a rod stuck down my throat. After tens of thousands of dollars of medical tests, there's an easy fix. Drinking a glass of water eases the ache in my chest before it doubles me over. Harder to fix were distinct memories of feeling my pain dismissed, not by doctors but by a crowd of onlookers. With good reason, I wondered if I would suddenly lose my sight. I worried that I would follow my uncles to an early grave.

When life hurts, we often find our pain brushed aside. People who have never been in our place—who have never felt a breeze blow through an open-back gown—have no idea how their words come across. Some of the worst brush-offs come when people tell us to "just pray about it," as if a few choice words aimed heavenward will instantly soothe our soul and make everything better. Truthfully, we never find peace through the mere act of praying. We get it from putting our trust in the God to whom we pray.

Calm

When the apostle Paul says that prayer will calm our anxieties, he might sound like yet another glib well-wisher. But there's more to the story.

We shouldn't overlook the backdrop to Paul's words. They appear in a letter to his cherished friends in Philippi, a privileged and sophisticated city in northern Greece. Citizens of this little slice of Rome spoke the language and enjoyed the laws of the empire's capital. Paul's upbeat letter contains more references to the word *joy* than any other Bible book.

This all might sound like the makings of a how-to book on creating and experiencing a carefree life. But Paul wrote his letter from jail (Philippians 1:12–26; 2:17), likely a period of imprisonment in Rome (Acts 28). He's facing a death sentence, pouring out the last drops of his life for God (Philippians 2:17). Yet as Paul suffers, he finds a shocking peace. He shares his secret of how we can live happy in some of life's nastiest surroundings. He says:

- "Do not be anxious about anything." Some concerns might be legitimate, but he clearly calls out our habit of letting anxiety control us. Then he explains how to master the worry that makes our hearts and minds spin.
- "In every situation, by prayer and petition, with thanksgiving, present your requests to God." The word for "prayer"

89

is more than a quick "bless this" or "fix that." It includes approaching God in worship, recognizing his greatness and goodness. "Petition" means expressing our specific needs. "Thanksgiving" means saying thanks for what he has already done.

- "And the peace of God, which transcends all understanding, will guard your hearts and your minds in Christ Jesus." God promises not just a little peace but an overflowing peace that protects all our feelings and thoughts.

Do you see the secret to peace? When we worship *and* express our need *and* say thanks, then we begin to experience God's calm.

Peace also comes from taking control of our minds, filling them with so many good thoughts that little room remains for anxiety to move in. Paul names the character of things that should occupy our thoughts. We are to think about whatever is

true ("valid," "reliable," "honest")

noble ("conforming to God's standards")

pure ("morally pure")

lovely ("pleasing," "agreeable")

admirable ("praiseworthy," "attractive," "ringing true to the highest standards")

And Paul finishes with more reasons to trust—promises clearly worth building into our prayers. Because of Jesus, we have strength for every circumstance. And as we survey all our real needs, we can count on God to meet them from his overflowing riches.

PHILIPPIANS 4:6

Do not be anxious about anything, but in every situation, by prayer and petition, with thanksgiving, present your requests to God.

I'm anxious about . . .

I nevertheless worship you because . . .

I need . . .

I'm grateful for . . .

PHILIPPIANS 4:7

And the peace of God, which transcends all understanding, will guard your hearts and your minds in Christ Jesus.

Train me to seek your peace when . . .

I'll stay focused on you by . . .

PHILIPPIANS 4:8

Finally, brothers and sisters, whatever is true, whatever is noble, whatever is right, whatever is pure, whatever is lovely, whatever is admirable—if anything is excellent or praiseworthy—think about such things.

I choose to clear my mind of . . .

I choose to fill my mind with . . .

PHILIPPIANS 4:9

Whatever you have learned or received or heard from me, or seen in me—put it into practice. And the God of peace will be with you.

Lead me to role models who . . .

I want to imitate . . .

PHILIPPIANS 4:12–13

I know what it is to be in need, and I know what it is to have plenty. I have learned the secret of being content in any and every situation, whether well fed or hungry, whether living in plenty or in want. I can do all this through him who gives me strength.

I lack . . .

I have . . .

I'll practice being content about . . .

With you in my life I can . . .

PHILIPPIANS 4:19

And my God will meet all your needs according to the riches of his glory in Christ Jesus.

I trust you to . . .

Reflect + Pray + Discuss

1. When has prayer helped calm your anxiety—or not?

2. Have you sensed others telling you to "just pray about it"? How did you respond?

3. What new ways of praying might help you experience peace?

9

surrender

And he withdrew from them about a stone's throw, and knelt down and prayed, saying, "Father, if you are willing, remove this cup from me. Nevertheless, not my will, but yours, be done."

Luke 22:41–42 ESV

What kept me going through the worst of my depression—what kept me alive when I wanted to die—was my wife, Lyn, and our kids. I love them. I care about their well-being now and into the future. Killing myself would have mercilessly and permanently sucked them into my own dark spiral.

For a long time I wished I would wake up one day and my pain would be gone. What I got instead was an ability to walk forward. As soon as I saw my doctor, I started taking an antidepressant. Pills don't make problems go away. But within weeks the meds made it significantly harder for my thoughts and emotions to travel down the same old desperate rut. For me medication was a crucial intervention and the start of getting well.

I found safe people among my family and friends, people who would love me despite the horrible unworthiness I felt. One was my editor, who fed me burritos and suggested I was ready to write this book and spill my guts for the benefit of others living with pain.

I learned to guard against adversaries happy to exploit my weakness. That sounds paranoid. But some people prefer to watch us lose so they can win, at the cost of relationships, health, or even life. It's completely unwise to let them have any idea what goes on inside us.

As my head got to a better place, I came to see that my feelings don't always reflect reality. I'm a creative, sometimes brooding thinker. The world inside my head often feels more real than the world I can see. I need others to help me evaluate people and situations to make sure I have my facts straight. I have to deal in reality.

I got back to trail running to force myself to focus on the here-and-now world of dirt and rocks and roots. I made myself pause and gawk when wild deer or turkeys crossed my path. That isn't the solution for everyone in pain. For me, exercise eventually took the place of meds.

I found hobbies to engage in for nothing but fun. Photography became my passion, and I created a happy space by surrounding myself with beautiful photos of people, places, and things I love. You can see some of my shots at kjphotos.zenfolio.com. I bought a telescope to calm me whenever my sleep turns restless. Even from the city the heavens declare God's glory.

And I prayed. I had pleaded with God for so long that I had run out of words. But I slowly, cautiously, deliberately wrote 4,500 prayers responding to every part of the Bible. Creating the *Pray the Scriptures Bible* was part of my healing.

Life has brought me an assortment of pains inward and outward. Some days I find them amusingly odd. But I know that my hurts are nothing compared to what others endure. I watch people suffer with far more serious medical conditions. Some die before they get better. Other individuals and families cope with severe mental illness. Some people I meet feel constant shame and guilt. Or there's no end to conflict and betrayal. Families unravel. Friendships break. I see people living with long-term unemployment and want. And what they all have in common is this: People who manage to walk forward through pain have all embraced a mission. They find a reason to push onward.

Mission

Hours before his crucifixion, Jesus went to the Mount of Olives, headed for a garden called Gethsemane, "The Olive Press," a place where ripe olives are crushed for their oil. That's what Jesus experienced there. He was a man caught between a rock and another rock.

In that garden Jesus knelt and pleaded with his heavenly Father, searching for an alternative plan for saving humankind, anything other than carrying every human sin to the cross. He prayed, "Father, if you are willing, remove this cup from me."

It's correct to see an epic struggle within Jesus. He felt such agony that his sweat was like great drops of blood. But to pour himself out in prayer was nothing new or unusual for Jesus. A chapter back—on Tuesday—Luke reports that "each day Jesus was teaching at the temple, and each evening he went out to spend the night on the hill called the Mount of Olives" (Luke 21:37 NIV). And right here—on Thursday evening—Luke says that "Jesus went out as usual to the Mount of Olives, and his disciples followed him" (22:39 NIV).

101

Going to the garden to talk with his Father was habit. There Jesus felt anguish. There he prayed. And there he surrendered, knowing exactly what lay ahead. Although he was innocent of wrongdoing, he would be arrested, beaten, and sentenced. His hands and feet would be nailed to a cross. He would die in agony and shame. Still, Jesus said yes. Not to the physical, psychological, or spiritual pain, but to his Father's plan. He prayed, "Father, if you are willing, remove this cup from me. Nevertheless, not my will, but yours, be done."

Forward

As Jesus went to the cross, he never thought suffering was fundamentally good. He never blessed the evil system that conspired against him. He never celebrated the toll of human wrongdoing. But he walked forward because he knew what was on the far side of the cross.

Jesus kept his mission at the front of his mind. He "humbled himself by becoming obedient to death—even death on a cross!" (Philippians 2:8 NIV). He "held on while wicked people were doing evil things to him" (Hebrews 12:3 NCV). He endured agony and shame "as if it were nothing" (v. 2 NCV) because of the joyful outcome he saw on the other side. His death and resurrection would reconnect God and humankind.

The core of my depression was this: I felt trapped. I was convinced I was immobilized by people, circumstances, and my own limitations. But knowing that God has a purpose for me, I found a way through my pain. I had a mission to live for. Even if I mattered to no one else in the world, my family needed me. So I surrendered. Not to my pain. To God. To his plan, insights, and timing. No matter what we suffer, as long as we walk with God, "trapped" is not a real thing. There is always a reason and a way to push forward.

LUKE 22:39–40

And he came out and went, as was his custom, to the Mount of Olives, and the disciples followed him. And when he came to the place, he said to them, "Pray that you may not enter into temptation."

When I feel pain, my habit is to . . .

Today I'll follow you to the garden. I feel . . .

Luke 22:41–42

And he withdrew from them about a stone's throw, and knelt down and prayed, saying, "Father, if you are willing, remove this cup from me. Nevertheless, not my will, but yours, be done."

I wish there was a way around my pain. I want . . .

I think you want . . .

I choose to . . .

LUKE 22:43–44

And there appeared to him an angel from heaven, strengthening him. And being in an agony he prayed more earnestly; and his sweat became like great drops of blood falling down to the ground.

Send me strength. I need . . .

Choosing to walk forward is hard. Show me how to . . .

LUKE 22:45–46

And when he rose from prayer, he came to the disciples and found them sleeping for sorrow, and he said to them, "Why are you sleeping? Rise and pray that you may not enter into temptation."

People grow weary of my pain. They . . .

I'm concerned about the people who do their best to support me. Give them . . .

Hebrews 12:1–2

Let us run with endurance the race that is set before us, looking to Jesus, the founder and perfecter of our faith, who for the joy that was set before him endured the cross, despising the shame, and is seated at the right hand of the throne of God.

I'll run the course you put before me. I will . . .

I will push forward because . . .

I won't let anything stop me, not even . . .

Reflect + Pray + Discuss

1. What might it mean for you to "despise" the pain you are suffering?

2. What does it look like to push ahead?

3. How does the example of Jesus motivate you?

10

hope

The Lord is my light and my salvation. Who is there
to fear? The Lord is my life's fortress. Who is there
to be afraid of?

Psalm 27:1 GOD'S WORD

The prophet Ezekiel lived among God's Old Testament people
at the worst of their worst. They had been dragged as prison-
ers a thousand miles east to the land of their enemies. There
in Babylon the people wailed bitterly, expressing their pain in
excruciating laments like Psalm 37. Not long after the people
arrived in exile, a few deceivers said everything would soon be
better, as if God would put them all on the next bus back home.
But God told everyone to settle in. They weren't going anywhere.
Most of them would live out their days in this alien land.

But God gave Ezekiel a vision. The prophet gazed across a
valley filled edge to edge with human bones. Apparently the

people had a habit of saying, "Our bones are dry, and our hope has vanished. We are completely destroyed" (Ezekiel 37:11).

Bones scattered across a wasteland. Hope gone. Complete ruin. What a picture of how we feel when life hurts.

God asked Ezekiel if the bones could be brought back to life. That question has an obvious answer. From a human perspective—of course not. But it was God asking. Ezekiel replied carefully. "Only you know, Almighty Lord," he said (v. 3). God can do anything. But would he?

The Lord gave Ezekiel a script to speak aloud to the bones. "I will cause breath to enter you," he declared, "and you will live. I will put ligaments on you, place muscles on you, and cover you with skin. I will put breath in you, and you will live. Then you will know that I am the Lord" (vv. 5–6). Then Ezekiel saw the bones come to life and stand on their feet (v. 10). Where there was death, God breathed fresh life.

Hope

When life hurts, do you have any hope for what lies ahead? What awaits you today, tomorrow, next year? When my doctor told me I didn't have to stay stuck in depression, I believed him. He ranks at the top of his profession. He's as honest and straightforward as anyone I know. I've never known him to blow smoke. I chose to let him into my darkest thoughts, and he said I could get better. His words inspired hope.

We usually use the word *hope* to mean "wish" or "want," as in "I wish I felt better" or "I want to win the lottery." We might or might not believe those things will happen. We might lay odds that they won't. But that isn't the essence of hope as Bible writers use the term. Hope is sure. It's a confident expectation. It's waiting with full trust that God's promises will come to pass. So the exiles could count on good things ahead when

110

God showed Ezekiel a valley of dead bones rattling back to life. They could take God at his word when he said, "I know the plans that I have for you. . . . They are plans for peace and not disaster, plans to give you a future filled with hope" (Jeremiah 29:11). God uttered those words thousands of years ago to his exiled people, but they still matter for us now. Hope is what keeps us moving ahead.

Ezekiel doesn't mention what happened after those bones stood up. But God added to his promise. He vowed to spring his people from their graves. His Spirit would fill them. One day they would again inhabit his land. Putting them back in the land implies they would live close to him (Ezekiel 37:12–14). Once they were as good as dead. Soon they would be people on the move.

Now

I'm back on a journey. Some days abound with intriguing situations and jaw-dropping scenery. Other days it's as if the world drags everything ugly up to the road so I can get a good look at it. As I look back at my winding path, those miles of severe depression are like a ghastly danger off in the distance. I know where it is and stay away. I purposely remember how bad it was so I never go back there. All in all, I have an idea where I'm headed, but I never know exactly what's around a curve or over a hill.

At the worst of my worst I couldn't imagine moving forward ever again. But I didn't have to live like that. My heart healed. My thinking cleared. Even when my body broke, it didn't push me back to despair. When I deal with crazy, persistent neurological symptoms now, they don't drag me over the edge. Most of all, I again have hope. The world is no longer a dark and scary place. With God in control, I expect a better future.

"Better" doesn't mean a life free from pain for me or anyone else. Some losses can't be recovered. Loved ones don't come back from the grave—for now. Our physical healings are often incomplete. They're always impermanent. We sometimes grieve lost months, seasons, even years. Our suffering marks everyone who loves us. And despite what some Christians claim, faith doesn't make everything instantly better.

For a long time I wished I would wake up and my pain would be gone. What I got instead was an ability to walk forward. I don't know what that means in your situation, but it's better than where you've been. It might be peace in the midst of anxiety. Or patience in imperfection. Or a new sense of God's presence. Or his surprising protection. Or his provision of exactly what you need. To live in hope means we are certain that something more awaits us.

The Bible abounds with examples of people who have walked this path ahead of us. We see snippets of their lives in places like Hebrews 11, a hall of fame for people known and unknown who chased after God. We get longer stories throughout the Old and New Testaments. Maybe the fullest portrait comes from the life of David. As you push forward on your own path, pray his words in Psalm 27. He starts by declaring that God is light and salvation. He tells of enemies waiting to tear him to pieces. He expresses his passionate intent to live near God. And then David concludes with these words:

> I believe that I will see the goodness of the Lord
> in this world of the living.
> Wait with hope for the Lord.
> Be strong, and let your heart be courageous.
> Yes, wait with hope for the Lord.

Be strong. Let your heart be courageous. Live confidently with hope in the Lord. You will yet see his goodness in the land of the living.

PSALM 27:1

> The Lord is my light and my salvation.
> Who is there to fear?
> The Lord is my life's fortress.
> Who is there to be afraid of?

You are . . .

I refuse to fear . . .

PSALM 27:2–3

> Evildoers closed in on me to tear me to pieces.
> My opponents and enemies stumbled and fell.
> Even though an army sets up camp against me,
> my heart will not be afraid.
> Even though a war breaks out against me,
> I will still have confidence in the Lord.

I'm surrounded by . . .

The worst that can happen is . . .

Even if all of life falls apart, I will . . .

Psalm 27:4

I have asked one thing from the Lord.
    This I will seek:
        to remain in the Lord's house all the days of my
            life
            in order to gaze at the Lord's beauty
                and to search for an answer in his temple.

I'll make you my highest priority by . . .

I want to be close to you because . . .

PSALM 27:5–7

He hides me in his shelter when there is trouble.
He keeps me hidden in his tent.
He sets me high on a rock.
Now my head will be raised above my enemies who
surround me.
I will offer sacrifices with shouts of joy in his tent.
I will sing and make music to praise the Lord.
Hear, O Lord, when I cry aloud.
Have pity on me, and answer me.

You have protected me from . . .

I will sing praises to you about . . .

116

PSALM 27:8–10

When you said,
"Seek my face,"
my heart said to you,
"O Lord, I will seek your face."
Do not hide your face from me.
Do not angrily turn me away.
You have been my help.
Do not leave me!
Do not abandon me, O God, my savior!
Even if my father and mother abandon me,
the Lord will take care of me.

You won't ever . . .

You're more faithful to me than . . .

PSALM 27:11–12

> Teach me your way, O Lord.
>> Lead me on a level path
>> because I have enemies who spy on me.
> Do not surrender me to the will of my opponents.
>> False witnesses have risen against me.
>> They breathe out violence.

I still have to deal with . . .

Don't let me be overwhelmed by . . .

PSALM 27:13–14

I believe that I will see the goodness of the Lord
  in this world of the living.
Wait with hope for the Lord.
    Be strong, and let your heart be courageous.
    Yes, wait with hope for the Lord.

I confidently expect . . .

Because I hope in you I will . . .

Reflect + Pray + Discuss

1. What is hope?

2. When have you been most hopeless?

3. How will hope enable you to walk forward right now?

Kevin Johnson is the creator of the first-of-its-kind *Pray the Scriptures Bible* and the bestselling author or co-author of more than fifty books and study Bibles for adults, students, and children. His training includes an MDiv from Fuller Theological Seminary and a BA in English and print journalism from the University of Wisconsin–River Falls. With a background as a youth worker, senior nonfiction book editor, and teaching pastor, he now leads Emmaus Road Church in metro Minneapolis. Kevin is married to Lyn, and they have three grown children.

Learn more at kevinjohnsonbooks.com.

More Guidance in Praying the Scriptures

This Bible—the first of its kind—is your tool to incorporating biblical prayer into your regular Bible reading and devotional time. It includes Scripture-specific prayers to be read and prayed alongside the Scriptures that inspired them, a guide to praying the Scriptures, an index of prayers that appear in Scripture, and a topical prayer guide.

Pray the Scriptures Bible by Kevin Johnson

Draw closer to God by praying His Word every day. With prayer-starter phrases to help you create your own Scripture prayers, as well as daily devotionals, Scripture texts, and questions for reflection, this forty-day journey will energize your prayer life!

Pray the Scriptures by Kevin Johnson